THEORY OF GAMES AS A TOOL FOR THE MORAL PHILOSOPHER

BY

R. B. BRAITHWAITE

*Knightbridge Professor of Moral Philosophy
in the University of Cambridge*

AN INAUGURAL LECTURE
DELIVERED IN CAMBRIDGE ON
2 DECEMBER 1954

D1597949

CAMBRIDGE
AT THE UNIVERSITY PRESS
1963

PUBLISHED BY
THE SYNDICS OF THE CAMBRIDGE UNIVERSITY PRESS

Bentley House, 200 Euston Road, London, N.W. 1
American Branch: 32 East 57th Street, New York 22, N.Y.
West African Office: P.O. Box 33, Ibadan, Nigeria

First printed 1955
Reprinted 1963

First printed in Great Britain at the University Press, Cambridge
Reprinted by offset-litho by
Lowe & Brydone (Printers) Ltd, London, N.W. 10

I T is a frequent complaint against academic moral philosophers that they inhabit an ivory tower where they meditate upon the analysis of ethical concepts or explore the logical semantics of the language of morals without ever descending to earth to apply their abstract studies in giving practical advice as to how to solve actual moral problems. The reply we academics usually make to this accusation is that our critics are confusing the function of an ethical philosopher with that of a moralist: the function of a moralist is to advise or to exhort, that of a philosopher to think about ethics, or, indeed, to think about thinking about ethics. But I, for one, am sufficiently sensitive to this criticism to be prepared to moralize about anything which my philosophizing has given me reason for moralizing about—especially when, as in the matter about which I shall venture to advise you today, the exposition of the reasons for the advice I shall offer as moralist are exactly the considerations which will be involved when, for a few moments towards the end of the lecture, I shall re-ascend the ivory tower to philosophize upon the ethical concepts I have employed.

The concept with which I shall be principally concerned is one which is given various names in different contexts—*Justice*, sometimes, in one of its many senses; *equitable distribution* in the context of welfare economics; *Égalité* if one is manning the barricades in its defence. I shall be very British and will call it *fair*

3

play or *fairness*. The situations in which it is involved are those in which we, as social beings, find ourselves every day of our lives. We cannot get what we want except by co-operating with other people whose wants are different from ours. It would be reasonable for Robinson Crusoe to aim simply at maximizing his own satisfaction while he was alone on his island. But when Man Friday arrived, co-operative action became possible, and in this Friday's wishes would have to be taken into account. Can the philosophical moralist give any advice to people with different aims as to how they may collaborate in common tasks so as to obtain maximum satisfaction compatible with fair distribution? I need not elaborate upon the practical importance of securing such collaboration in all spheres of life, domestic, social, national, international.

Moral philosophers have, for the most part, ignored this question. They have supposed that, unless people can agree at any rate upon the proximate ends which they all wish to pursue, no rational basis for common action is possible. Many philosophers have pointed out that, however wide a divergence there may be about ultimate ends, there is a large measure of agreement as to proximate ends (such as the maintenance of law and order, or the preservation of individual freedom) which are necessary conditions for many different ultimate ends, so that the matter is not quite as hopeless as it appears to be. But they have left any serious study of the question to the welfare economists who, heirs of the Utilitarian tradition, have evolved theories of production and distribution based upon the assumption that the ends

4

desired by different people—their 'utilities'—can be compared with one another in terms of common units (frequently monetary units) which can be transferred from one person to another. Welfare economists, however, whether they regard themselves as describing the actual working of an economic system or as prescribing a more ideal functioning, have come in for a great deal of criticism recently from their fellow-economists based largely upon the impossibility of any inter-personal comparison of utilities. So many economists today are as negative in their attitude to our problem as are the philosophers—though with more excuse, for they at least have tried out one line of approach.

I propose today to try another line of attack, suggested to me by thinking about the new mathematical discipline called Theory of Games. Though this approach will presuppose that each person can compare his own preferences for alternative courses of action, it will not presuppose that the preference scale of one person can be compared with that of another; a method of inter-personal comparison will arise naturally in the course of the argument. My treatment will be ethically neutral between the collaborating parties; it will not suppose that one code of values is better than any other, nor will it require that any of the collaborators should attempt to convert his colleagues to his own system of valuation. The recommendations which I shall make for sharing fairly the proceeds of collaboration will therefore be *amoral* in the sense that they will not be based upon any first-order moral principles; but the recommendations themselves will constitute what may be called second-order moral principles giving criteria for *good sense*, *prudence* and *fairness*, principles in some way analogous to the 'supplementary Principle' for 'Just distribution of happiness' which Henry Sidgwick, my 'great-grandfather' in this Knightbridge Chair, found necessary to sweeten the pure milk of the Utilitarian gospel.[1]

After these preliminaries, let me attack the problem directly. But first I must limit my objective to situations in which there are only two persons concerned in the collaboration. Although this is a serious limitation, the two-person situation covers more than may appear at first sight, since 'person' may be taken in the extended legal sense in which a corporate body— a University, a Company, a State, any social group which decides and acts collectively—may be said to be a person. Why it is necessary to start with the two-person case is that, if a group of more than two are involved, the possibility arises of forming subgroups within the group—cabals, coalitions, trusts, cartels, etc.—with mutual assistance pacts designed to promote the interests of the subgroup at the expense of those outside it. This possibility introduces serious complications into the problem, how serious has been shown by the Games Theorists. So my limitation to two persons is essential to my treatment.

But my second limitation is made purely for expository convenience. My two persons—let us call them Luke and Matthew (L and M)—will be supposed each to have only two possible ways of acting in the collaboration situation: Luke can act either in one way or in one other; Matthew can act either in one way or in one other. This limitation is inessential, since the mathematics can be straightforwardly, though laboriously, extended to cover situations in which each collaborator has the same finite number n of possible ways of acting.[2] But to expound the $n \times n$ case would require covering several blackboards with sets of simultaneous equations, whereas in the 2×2 case simple geometrical arguments can take the place of heavy algebra. So I shall limit myself in this lecture to the case in which Luke has two possible ways of acting, L_1 and L_2, and Matthew has two possible ways, M_1 and M_2, so that the results of their combined actions may be represented by a four-square table in which Luke has the choice between the upper and the lower row, and Matthew the choice between the left-hand and the right-hand column, and where the four τ's represent the outcomes of the four combinations of these choices:

| | M chooses between | |
	M_1	M_2
L_1	τ_{11}	τ_{12}
L_2	τ_{21}	τ_{22}

L chooses between

But you will probably prefer to think about the *pure invariant casuistry of two-person 2×2 fair collaboration* in terms of its application to a concrete example, and I shall continue my discussion entirely in terms of this example. I shall try to make it as realistic as possible, but of course various simplifying assumptions will have to be introduced in order that the example may be paradigmatic of the collaboration situation in general.

Suppose that Luke and Matthew are both bachelors, and occupy flats in a house which has been converted into two flats by an architect who had ignored all considerations of acoustics. Suppose that Luke can hear everything louder than a conversation that takes place in Matthew's flat, and vice versa; but that sounds in the two flats do not penetrate outside the house. Suppose that it is legally impossible for either to prevent the other from making as much noise as he wishes, and economically or sociologically impossible for either to move elsewhere. Suppose further that each of them has only the hour from 9 to 10 in the evening for recreation, and that it is impossible for either to change to another time. Suppose that Luke's form of recreation is to play classical music on the piano for an hour at a time, and that Matthew's amusement is to improvise jazz on the trumpet for an hour at once. And suppose that whether or not either of them performs on one evening has no influence, one way or the other, upon the desires of either of them to perform on any other evening; so that each evening's happenings can be treated independently. Suppose that the satisfaction each derives from playing his instrument for the hour is affected, one way or the other, by whether or not the other is also playing; in radio language, there is 'interference' between them,

8

positive or negative. Suppose that they put to me the problem: Can any plausible principle be devised stating how they should divide the proportion of days on which both of them play (τ_{11}), Luke alone plays (τ_{12}), Matthew alone plays (τ_{21}), neither play (τ_{22}), so as to obtain maximum production of satisfaction compatible with fair distribution?

The relevant data will be the extents of the preferences of each for the four alternatives. We will suppose that Luke's first preference is for him alone to play (τ_{12}), his second preference is for Matthew alone to play (τ_{21}) (since he quite likes hearing jazz when he is not playing himself), his third preference for neither to play (τ_{22}), while the thing he likes least is for Matthew to trumpet while he himself is playing the piano (τ_{11}). But, except in the obvious cases, a mere ranking of Luke's preferences in an order of preference is not a strong enough premiss. In order to be able to say much of interest, it is necessary to assign numerical values, not to Luke's preferences themselves, but to the ratios of his relative preferences for one outcome rather than for another. This can be done in the following manner. Suppose that Luke has no preference, one way or the other, between the two possibilities (a) of both of them always remaining silent, and (b) of Matthew alone playing on one-third of the evenings, and of their both playing on two-thirds of the evenings, on the average. Luke's indifference between τ_{22} and what amounts to a probability combination of τ_{21} with probability $1/3$ and τ_{11} with probability $2/3$, can be used to define what is meant by saying that the extent to which Luke prefers

τ_{21} to τ_{22} is twice the extent to which he prefers τ_{22} to τ_{11}. Suppose further than Luke is indifferent between the two possibilities (a) of both always remaining silent and (c) of himself alone playing on one-sixth of the evenings and of them both playing on five-sixths of the evenings, on the average. This will similarly determine that the extent to which Luke prefers τ_{12} to τ_{22} is five times the extent to which he prefers τ_{22} to τ_{11}. These two ratios will enable a scale of numbers to be assigned in a consistent way to Luke's valuations of the four alternatives and of all probability combinations of them, so that his preferences can be *measured* in the weak sense of measurement in which both the zero and the unit of measurement are arbitrarily chosen. This weak sense is that in which temperatures are measured by thermometers graduated according to, for example, the Centigrade scale. It implies that any result we get by using the scale of numbers measuring Luke's valuations must be unchanged if we select a different zero and a different unit for the scale, just as any scientific law about temperatures must be expressible indifferently in degrees Centigrade or in degrees Fahrenheit. In mathematical language, the only properties of the numbers that can be relevant are those which are invariant with respect to any linear transformation $x' = ax + b$ with a positive. When we represent, as it will be convenient to do, Luke's valuations by points along a straight line, what is determined by the weak measurement is merely the ratios of the distances between the points, so that everything we want to say about the points must be invariant for any uniform translation of the points along the line, and for any uniform expansion or contraction of the line, i.e. for any change in the zero point or in the unit of the scale.

This weak method of measuring preferences, by equating the number to be assigned to one valuation with the number to be assigned to a probability combination of two or more valuations, is implicit in the use made of the notion of *mathematical expectation* by writers on probability since the time of Leibniz; it appears explicitly in F. P. Ramsey's suggestions for a calculus of degrees of belief read to the Cambridge Moral Science Club in 1926 and published post-humously in 1931. Its appropriateness has been the subject of a great deal of discussion in recent economic literature since von Neumann and Morgenstern elaborated it in 1944 for use in Theory of Games, the discussion centring round the fact that the prob-ability-combination-indifference method (as I shall call it) does not allow for the love of gambling, or of insurance, for its own sake. But whether or not the method is altogether suitable for measuring pre-ferences with respect to possible alternatives on a unique, unrepeatable occasion, e.g. if Luke and Matthew are birds of passage and are touching down in the flats on one evening only, it is the obvious way to measure their preferences if any one evening may be regarded as one of a long series of evenings in each of which the relevant conditions are exactly the same. So I shall adopt the probability-combination-indif-ference method without further question; no other method will allow of the use of Theory-of-Games techniques.

This method of measuring preferences, it must be emphasized, does not presuppose anything like the adding together of separate units of happiness which has been such an excellent cudgel with which to beat Utilitarianism in its earlier forms. It will be convenient, and a proper tribute to the economists, to refer to the numbers, chosen in accordance with the probability-combination-indifference method to measure Luke's valuations, as L-*utilities*. But to use this language is not to attach any special significance to a zero L-utility or to a unit L-utility; any result obtained will be independent of how the unit and zero are assigned; it will depend only upon the ratios in which the L-utility differences stand to one another.

If we assign M-utilities in the same way to measure Matthew's valuations, we can represent (as in Diagram I, p. 13) the pairs of valuations of the four possible outcomes of the collaboration situation by four outcome points (the four *base points*) on a Cartesian plane, where for each outcome point the horizontal or x co-ordinate represents Luke's valuation and the vertical or y co-ordinate Matthew's valuation of the outcome represented by the outcome point. Luke will wish to secure that the outcome point jointly chosen should be as far to the right as possible, Matthew that it should be as high up as possible. Since the origin of the co-ordinates and the scales along both the horizontal and the vertical axes are arbitrary, the only geometrical properties that can be relevant are those which are unchanged if the figure is moved without rotation or if it is expanded or contracted along either or both the axes. To assist in appreciating

this invariance the irrelevant axes of co-ordinates
have deliberately not been marked in all the remaining diagrams: the diagrams must also be supposed
to be stretchable in any uniform way provided only
that vertical lines remain vertical and horizontal lines
horizontal—as indicated by the direction indicator
on each diagram. The requirement that the relevant

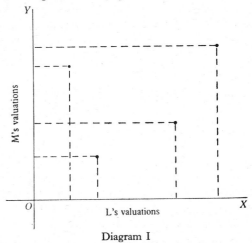

Diagram I

properties should be invariant with respect to a
deformation along one axis alone will ensure that we
are not surreptitiously relating the arbitrary L-
utility unit with the separately arbitrary M-utility
unit; my treatment presupposes a comparison of
L-utilities with one another, and of M-utilities with
one another, but it does not presuppose any comparison of L-utilities with M-utilities, though such a
comparison will be introduced in the argument. In
economists' language, our geometrical representation

does not presuppose any inter-personal comparison of utilities by means of a unit of utility common to both Luke and Matthew, still less any possibility of transference of units of utility from one to the other. Thus it avoids the most serious criticism levelled against the assumptions of welfare economics.

It also escapes from another criticism in that it is able to allow for envy, malice and all uncharitableness. For we shall suppose that Luke knows Matthew's preference scale, and vice versa. If Matthew has constructed his preference scale in the first instance without considering Luke's valuations, he is at perfect liberty to modify it when he knows these. Thus it may relatively diminish his satisfaction in trumpeting while Luke is silent if he knows how much Luke would enjoy playing the piano. Or, if he is a disagreeable man, the prospect of thwarting Luke may increase his satisfaction. We will suppose that these adjustments have all been made, so that the L-utilities measure Luke's preferences and the M-utilities measure Matthew's preferences when each knows the other's valuations.

In attacking the problem we must distinguish different kinds of cases, which can be specified by reference to the shapes of the two-dimensional figures.

The simplest kind is that in which (as in Diagram I) one of the four base points lies both to the right of and above each of the other three base points. Here the outcome corresponding to this base point will be preferred by both Luke and Matthew to any other outcome; the only *sensible* plan is for them to agree together to choose those actions which will jointly yield this result. For example, if Luke and Matthew are both so unselfish that each prefers playing his instrument when the other is similarly enjoying himself to all the other three alternatives, clearly they should both play every evening. This kind of case will be called that of *wholly non-competitive collaboration*; there is no conflict between the interests of the collaborators, and no difficulty whatever in recommending what is good sense for both of them to do.

The next most simple kind of case is the opposite—the *wholly competitive* situation—in which Luke's and Matthew's interests are directly opposed. This is represented geometrically, as in Diagram II (p. 18), by the four base points lying on a straight line sloping downwards from left to right. Luke wants his choice to result in a point as far to the right as possible, and Matthew wants his choice to result in one as high up as possible; so their pulls act along the line in opposite directions.

Now the simplest paradigm for a wholly competitive situation is a game played for stakes between two players, e.g. chess, two-handed poker; and since the mathematical concepts have been developed in connexion with such games the mathematical discipline is known as Theory of Games. Though this theory employs, it is quite distinct from Theory of Probability, which since the seventeenth century has been used to calculate the chances and the mathematical expectations in games of chance; the games with which Theory of Games is concerned, though they may include chance factors (as in bridge or poker), are essentially games of intellectual skill, games of strategy, *Gesellschaftsspiele, jeux où intervient l'habilité des joueurs*. Theory of Games is concerned with calculating what is the 'best' strategy for playing such a game, where a precise meaning is given to the notion of *best strategy*. It originated in the minds of two of the greatest living mathematicians. Émile Borel in 1921 thought of some of its basic ideas and saw their applicability to problems of economics; but he was held up by inability to establish the mathematically fundamental theorem. John von Neumann independently developed the theory, proving the fundamental theorem, in 1928; and in 1944, jointly with the economist Oskar Morgenstern, he expounded the theory in a treatise *Theory of Games and Economic Behavior*, which rapidly attained the status of a classic. The part of this book which deals with strategic games between two persons with directly opposed interests, each of whom has a finite number of possible strategies—what are called 'two-person zero-sum finite games'—proves that there is a best strategy for each player, and, in games analogous to the collaboration situations which we are considering, in which each player has the choice of only two moves, these best strategies are calculated. The treatment of von Neumann and Morgenstern, in terms of monetary stakes, limits itself to situations in which the gain to the winner can be equated to the loss to the loser; but it may be straightforwardly generalized to apply to all wholly competitive situations. I will expound the straightforward generalization by reference to its geometrical representation, and (except for the useful term *strategy*) shall not use Theory-of-Games language.

The various cases of the wholly competitive kind fall into two types. The first type comprises cases in which Luke will gain by choosing one strategy rather than the other, whatever strategy Matthew may choose. Here it is clearly most *prudent* for Luke to choose that strategy, and for Matthew to choose his strategy on the assumption that Luke will make that choice. The strategies chosen in this way, one by Luke, one by Matthew, I shall call *prudential strategies*. And similarly if it is Matthew who has one certainly advantageous choice.

The second type, however, when neither has a certainly advantageous choice, is intellectually the exciting one. Suppose that Luke's preference scale is as has been stated (pp. 9 f.), so that it is representable from left to right along the horizontal axis by points corresponding to Luke's valuations, where the intervals between the points stand in the ratios 1 to 2 to 3. Suppose now that Matthew gets no intrinsic enjoyment, positive or negative, from playing the trumpet, whether or not Luke is also playing, but that, actuated purely by malice, he trumpets only 'to annoy, Because he knows it teases'. His preference scale will then be represented along the vertical axis by points in the reverse ascending order with intervals standing in the ratios 3 to 2 to 1, so that the two-dimensional figure (Diagram II) will have the four base points lying on a downward-sloping straight line. The question is, how should Luke act so as to benefit as much as possible despite Matthew's malice? And how should Matthew act so as to annoy Luke as much as possible?

Von Neumann recommends that Luke should play the piano one evening in four on the average, choosing the days he shall play by a suitable chance-device (e.g. by drawing a card from a shuffled whist pack and playing the piano if the card drawn is a spade). Elementary algebra will show that by adopting this *mixed strategy* (as von Neumann calls it) the average L-utility, averaged over a long run, that Luke will obtain will be the same whatever strategy of annoy-

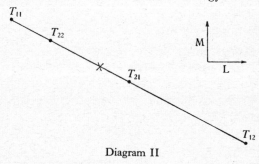

Diagram II

ance Matthew adopts. The corresponding recommendation to Matthew is that he should trumpet on the average five evenings in eight, choosing his trumpeting days by a suitable chance-device, by which means Matthew will secure that over the long run Luke will be equally annoyed, and he himself will derive the same malicious satisfaction, whatever strategy of evasion Luke employs.

These mixed strategies, like the prudential strategies in the first type of wholly competitive situation, are certainly the most *prudent* for Luke and Matthew to adopt. For each of these by adopting his *prudential strategy* (as I shall also call the mixed strategy recommended by von Neumann for the second type of situation) will make himself independent of the behaviour of the other; he will, over the long run, secure exactly the same utility to himself however his opponent chooses to act, and this utility will be the maximum utility which he can be quite certain of obtaining. The difference between using the prudential strategy in a situation of the first type and using the prudential strategy in one of the second type is that in the first type the prudential strategy is *pure* (i.e. not a probability combination of strategies), and it will secure to its user a utility which is not less and which may be more than the maximum utility which his opponent cannot prevent him from obtaining, whereas in the second type the prudential strategy, which is mixed, will always secure for him exactly this maximum. Since in the wholly competitive situation, whether of the first or of the second type, the interests of the two parties are directly opposed so that it is impossible for both of them simultaneously to improve upon what they would obtain by using prudential strategies, von Neumann has good reason, I think, for calling the prudential strategy for each of them his *best* strategy, and in calling the recommendation to both parties to use their prudential strategies a *solution* of the problem as to how it is rational to act in such a situation— though I myself shall not use these somewhat question-begging terms.

The insight that, by recommending mixed strategies (i.e. probability combinations of pure strategies) in some wholly competitive situations, it is possible to specify a plausible sense of *best*, equivalent in these contexts to *most prudent*, in which it can be proved that each party in every wholly competitive situation has a best strategy, is the fundamental idea in von Neumann's theory. Like most insights of genius, it is as simple as it is illuminating—though the mathematics required to establish the existence of best strategies in cases more complicated than the 2×2 case is highly sophisticated.

In the figure representing a wholly competitive situation, the four base points, and all probability combinations of them, lie on the same downward-sloping straight line, and there is no attainable position which is both to the right of and above the prudentially obtainable point (marked with a cross on Diagram II). There is thus no *co-operators' surplus* that might be shared if Luke and Matthew agreed between themselves not to adopt prudential strategies. There is, however, such a co-operators' surplus in the general case which is neither wholly competitive nor wholly non-competitive, and which is represented (as in Diagrams III–V) by a figure in which the four base points form a quadrangle with no corner to the right of and above all the other three. Here von Neumann's mathematics proves that there will be a prudential strategy for each collaborator, one which will secure for him the maximum benefit which is compatible with any choice of strategy by the other; but throws no light upon how the co-operators' surplus can be fairly shared. So von Neumann is unable to make any recommendation to the collaborators except that the strategy to be adopted by each of them should secure at least as much as would be secured by using his prudential strategy. For each of them the prudential strategy puts a lower bound to an outcome that would be acceptable to him, but no upper bound.

Though the theory of the wholly competitive situation (the zero-sum two-person game) is pretty completely explored, the theory of the general case of collaboration (the non-zero-sum two-person game) is almost virgin forest. Two pioneers, John Nash and Howard Raiffa, have recently attempted to cut tracks through this forest. Nash has hacked out a bold path, and has conducted two other economists down it (on the quest for solutions of problems of duopoly); but his path seems to me to go in a manifestly wrong direction. Independently of him, Raiffa has cut several openings in the forest, including Nash's path, but does not think any of them attractive enough to put his faith in. The limited exploration of mine which I shall now report to you—limited in that I am confining myself in this lecture to the case in which there are only two pure strategies open to each of the collaborators, whereas Nash's and Raiffa's treatments consider the most general cases, finite and infinite— owes much to my two predecessors, and in particular to Raiffa, one of whose openings in the forest I shall cut a new way into.[3]

I shall have time today to consider in detail only one typical case of collaboration which is partly but only partly competitive. It will be exemplified by the case in which Luke's preferences are represented along the horizontal axis as before, while Matthew's

preferences are represented along the vertical axis
by points in ascending order corresponding to his

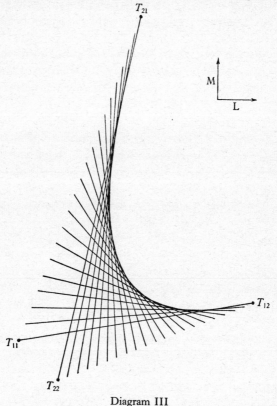

Diagram III

valuations of τ_{22}, τ_{11}, τ_{12}, τ_{21} in that order, where the
distances between the points stand in the ratios 1 to
1 to 7. (I have chosen these ratios so that there should
be no irrelevant symmetries in the figure.) Matthew,
that is to say, has as first preference his playing the

trumpet while Luke is silent, his second preference Luke's alone playing, his third preference both of them playing, while the thing he likes least is that neither of them should play (since he likes a cheerful noise about the house). And the interval between his first preference and his second preference, measured by the probability-combination-indifference method, is seven times the interval between his second and third preferences, which is equal to the interval between his third and last preferences. The four base-point figure representing this example is shown on Diagrams III–V, where it must always be borne in mind that the sizes of the units of measurement, both horizontal and vertical, are irrelevant and that the horizontal and vertical units are independent of one another.

Look now at Diagram III (p. 22). Suppose that Luke adopts the pure strategy L_1, of playing the piano every evening. Matthew is at liberty to adopt either of his two pure strategies, M_1 or M_2, or any probability combination of them; he can, that is, choose the proportion of evenings on which to trumpet. Since probability combinations are linear functions, Luke's pure strategy L_1 will be represented on the figure by the straight-line segment joining T_{11}, the leftmost point on the figure, to T_{12}, the rightmost point. Luke's pure strategy L_2, of never playing the piano, will similarly be represented by the line segment joining T_{21}, the highest point on the figure, to T_{22}, the lowest point. Luke's mixed strategies, which are probability combinations of L_1 and L_2, will be represented by line segments joining points equidistantly spaced along the line $T_{11}T_{21}$ to corresponding points equidistantly spaced along the line $T_{12}T_{22}$. These line segments form what geometers call a *scroll*. Twenty-one members of this scroll are shown in Diagram III, the two extreme lines representing the two pure strategies, the nineteen intermediate lines mixed strategies at 5% probability intervals. The line of the scroll which is vertical represents Luke's prudential strategy; no recommendation which I might make would be acceptable to him if he could gain more by using this strategy. Luke has an infinite number of strategies to choose from—an infinite number, since he can decide to mix his two pure strategies in any probability combination, i.e. he can select any proportion of evenings on which to play the piano—and his choice of one of these strategies corresponds to a choice on Diagram III of one out of the infinite number of line segments of which the twenty-one drawn form a sample.

Now look at Diagram IV (p. 25). This similarly shows twenty-one members of the scroll representing Matthew's strategies. The upper extreme line represents his pure strategy of playing the trumpet every evening, the lower extreme line his pure strategy of never playing, and the nineteen intermediate lines his mixed strategies of playing on a proportion of the evenings, proportions of 5%, 10%, ..., 95% respectively. The line of the scroll which is horizontal represents Matthew's prudential strategy. His choice of one out of the infinite number of strategies open to him (for he can decide the proportion of

evenings upon which he will trumpet) corresponds to
a choice on Diagram IV of one of the infinite number

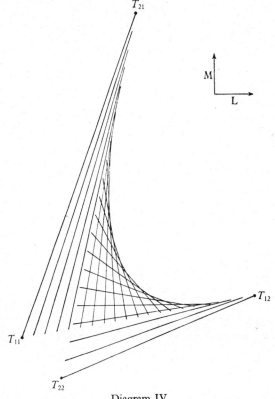

Diagram IV

of line segments of which the twenty-one drawn form
a sample.

The collaboration situation will be represented by
a superposition of one of the diagrams upon the other;
Luke will choose one of the line segments from

Diagram III, and Matthew one from Diagram IV, and the outcome will be represented by the point on the conflated diagram where these two lines intersect. Von Neumann's lower bound to an acceptable solution determines that no recommendation to Luke will be acceptable to him if it would result in the outcome point lying to the left of the vertical line segment of Diagram III, and that no recommendation to Matthew will be acceptable to him if it would result in the outcome point lying below the horizontal line segment of Diagram IV. Thus to be acceptable to both, the recommended strategies must jointly yield an outcome point lying to the right of and above these two lines respectively.

I have drawn the two diagrams separately, and each with many lines, both so that you may satisfy yourselves that the boundaries of the two figures are the same, and also so that you may inspect the shape of the curve which in each case forms the greater part of the upper right-hand boundary. That the boundaries of the two figures are the same is an obvious consequence of their method of construction, since when the two figures are conflated every line of Diagram III must intersect every line of Diagram IV. It is not obvious from the method of construction what the shape of the curved part of the boundary must be; but geometry will prove that it is a *parabola*. (The proof is exceedingly simple if methods of projective geometry are used.[4]) This parabola is the parabola— the unique parabola—which touches the four lines representing the four pure strategies concerned (each line segment being taken as infinitely extended in both directions). Every line representing a mixed strategy, either of Luke's or of Matthew's or of both, also touches the parabola. In geometrical language the parabola is the *envelope* of all the strategy lines. The scroll of Luke's strategy lines and the scroll of Matthew's strategy lines each forms a part of the total scroll of lines enveloping the parabola; if Luke's scroll and Matthew's scroll overlap (as they do in the case we are considering), they are identical where they overlap. The choices of strategy may then be converted into choices of points on the parabola; Luke can choose any point on the parabola lying between the points where his two pure strategy lines touch the parabola, and Matthew can do likewise. If the points they choose on the parabola are the same, that point is the outcome point; if they are different, the outcome point is the intersection of the tangents to the parabola at the two points.

The fundamental idea of the argument I shall now present to you rests upon the discovery that the logic of the general collaboration situation is isomorphic with the geometry of a parabola regarded as an envelope of lines (a line parabola or parabola-scroll, as geometers call it), the parabola being uniquely determined by the four pure strategies available to the collaborators. The importance of the parabola arises from the fact that a definite direction is associated with it, namely, the direction of its axis; this direction, which is not an arbitrary one since it arises naturally out of the intrinsic logic of the situation, will give a method of comparing the preference scales of the two collaborators. And if this can be done, it will be possible to measure (by the probability-combination-indifference method) the relative advantage Luke has over Matthew, or Matthew over Luke, for the different possible outcomes, and so to reduce the difficult part of the problem to that of a situation in which Luke will be trying to increase, and Matthew to decrease, this relative advantage, which is a wholly competitive situation.

The neither wholly competitive nor wholly non-competitive collaboration between Luke and Matthew may thus be regarded as a competition between them for relative advantage, followed by a wholly non-competitive collaboration between them for maximizing their utilities on condition that the relative advantage given by the prudential strategy recommendation for the wholly competitive part of the situation is preserved. In economic language, the problem of fair distribution will first be solved, and its solution will enable us to solve the problem, otherwise insoluble, of how production should be maximized.

To work this out in our example is easy. Look at Diagram V (p. 29), where the cross-hatched figure corresponds to the scroll figures of Diagrams III and IV. Imagine a beam of lines ruled across the figure, all parallel to the axis of the parabola (three such lines are shown on Diagram V). Let us take the logic of the situation as determining that Luke's relative advantage over Matthew is constant along each line of the beam. The lines, that is, are contour lines of constant relative advantage: I will call them *isorrhopes*. Luke will aim at increasing his relative advantage by securing an outcome point lying on an isorrhope as far to the right as possible, Matthew will aim at decreasing Luke's relative advantage by securing an

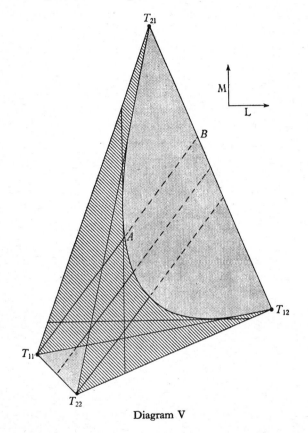

Diagram V

outcome point lying on an isorrhope as high, and therefore as far to the left, as possible. Thus they will directly compete for the isorrhopes. The wholly competitive situation of our example will be one of the first type (p. 17). The prudential strategy for Matthew in this competition is to choose his pure strategy M_1, of playing the trumpet every evening, since he will thereby obtain an isorrhope higher than one which he can obtain by any other strategy, whatever be the strategy chosen by Luke. The prudential strategy for Luke is to assume that Matthew will choose M_1, and consequently to choose L_1, that of playing the piano every evening. Luke will thereby secure that the isorrhope will be the rightmost of all those made possible for him by Matthew's choice of M_1. The outcome point resulting from each choosing his prudential strategy in the isorrhopic competition is T_{11}, the base point farthest to the left; each of them will play his instrument every evening.

But this outcome, which would result from each of them aiming at maximizing his relative advantage over the other, is not what either of them wants. For, since the outcome point T_{11} is to the left of the vertical tangent to the parabola and below the horizontal tangent, it is a worse result for each of them than would have resulted from each of them using his prudential strategy in the original collaboration and thus obtaining von Neumann's lower bound to an acceptable solution. What each was really coveting in the isorrhopic competition was the most advantageous isorrhope, and the isorrhope obtained by their each choosing the strategy prudential for this purpose is the highest one shown on Diagram V; let us call it the *prudential isorrhope*. It is unfortunate for both of them that the strategies which yield the prudential isorrhope also determine the outcome point as being the point which is both leftmost and lowest on this isorrhope, and so is least favourable to both. But if each of them will agree that the result of their isorrhopic competition has settled that, wherever the fair outcome point lies, it must lie on the prudential isorrhope, all that is left of the problem is that of collaborating to secure the best possible outcome point on this isorrhope. Since the isorrhope slopes upwards from left to right, this collaboration is wholly noncompetitive; both of them prefer a point as far up the isorrhope as possible, and the top end of the isorrhope where it runs into the upper right-hand frontier of the region of possible outcome points will be the point preferred. In our example this point (marked A on Diagram V) lies on the parabola; to attain it each collaborator must choose the mixed strategy represented by the tangent to the parabola at this point. Luke's strategy will then be to play the piano on the average 23 evenings out of 68, Matthew's strategy will be to trumpet on the average 59 evenings out of 104; and if they consult me as to what strategies to adopt, I shall provisionally recommend these strategies to them jointly, delivering this lecture to them as my reason for this recommendation.

Please understand that I should not recommend these strategies on the ground that they are the most prudent in the sense that they will secure to each the maximum advantage which is compatible with complete ignorance as to how the other will act. The prudential strategies are, as we have seen, for Luke to select as his strategy line the vertical tangent and for

Matthew to select the horizontal tangent; they will each in this case profit less than if they had taken my advice. Prudence alone will enable no inroads to be made upon the co-operators' surplus; to do that sufficient mutual confidence is required for Luke and Matthew to come to an agreement that they should each play their instruments in specified proportions, so that Luke can rely upon Matthew's not trumpeting more than 59/104ths of the time if Luke confines his playing to 23/68ths of the time, and vice versa.

But the merit in my eyes of the conjunction of strategies which I should provisionally recommend to them is that, since it is based upon the 'balance of power' between them, it requires the least degree of mutual confidence. For if Matthew, having agreed with Luke that they will both use the mixed strategies which I have recommended, breaks his word and changes his strategy from the agreed one to one more favourable to himself, on the assumption that Luke will stick to the one agreed, Luke will counter by the reverse policy when he discovers what Matthew is doing. If Matthew turns his strategy line round clockwise from the agreed tangent, thinking that this will be to his advantage, Luke will turn his strategy line round counter-clockwise, which will more than counter-balance any advantage Matthew would have gained. If they continue turning their strategy lines in opposite directions, they will end up with the pure strategies of both playing their instruments every evening, with T_{11} as outcome point. I shall then point out to them that each has exactly the same advantage or disadvantage over the other as he had before the agreement was broken, since T_{11} and the agreement point A lie on the same isorrhope (indeed this was how the agreement point was fixed), and ask them to consider whether it is really worth their while conducting a war whose result is to the disadvantage of both parties. By this means I should hope to get them to accept the fact that, the prudential isorrhope having been settled by purely competitive considerations, it would be foolish for them not to agree, and hold to an agreement, to secure the outcome point on this isorrhope most favourable to both.

I have called my recommendation to choose strategies yielding as outcome point the point A where the prudential isorrhope intersects the parabola a *provisional* recommendation. This is because, once I have got Luke and Matthew to agree to co-operate in implementing it, I can then suggest a method by which they can together improve on it. For my provisional recommendation was for Luke to play the piano 23/68ths of the time, and for Matthew to play the trumpet 59/104ths of the time, on the average. This will result in their either both playing or both not playing on approximately 48% of the evenings; so nearly half the recreation time will be spent less enjoyably by each of them than it need have been, since they both put these two alternatives in the lower halves of their scales of preference. So I shall suggest that they can eliminate this wasted time by not choosing their musical evenings independently (though in an agreed proportion) but by co-operating in dividing the evenings into those on which Luke plays the piano while Matthew is silent, and those on which Matthew trumpets while Luke is silent. Suppose they would have been using separate packs of cards—Luke a pack of 68 cards, 23 of them marked with an L, Matthew a pack of 104 cards, 59 of them marked with an M—to determine whether or not each will play his instrument on any one evening— Luke to play if he draws an L-marked card from his pack, Matthew to play if he draws an M-marked card from his pack. My suggestion is that they should throw away their separate packs, and use instead a common pack of cards marked either L or M but not both, and should settle on each occasion which of them should play and which should be silent by one draw from this common pack.

By using a common chance-device to settle what I will call their *coupled strategy*, Luke and Matthew together will be able to obtain outcome points lying outside the region to which use of separate strategies, pure or mixed, would have restricted them (the *paired-strategies region*, cross-hatched on Diagram V). The region available with the use of a coupled strategy as well as paired strategies (the *total strategic region*) is what geometers call the 'convex hull' of their paired-strategies region (it is also in fact the convex hull of their paired-pure-strategies region); in our example it is the region lying on or inside the quadrangle whose vertices are the four base points T_{11}, T_{21}, T_{12}, T_{22}. (The part of the total strategic region outside the paired-strategies region is shown as stippled on Diagram V.) The only new part of this quadrangle of interest to Luke and Matthew will be its upper right-

34

hand boundary line, the line $T_{21}T_{12}$, which is the locus of the outcome points that would result from their agreeing to settle the proportions of the two alternatives of each alone playing his instrument by the use of a common chance-device. How should this common chance-device be adjusted so that the division of time should be fair? My recommendation will be that it should be adjusted so that the resulting outcome point on the boundary line $T_{21}T_{12}$ is the point (marked B on Diagram V) where this line is cut by the upward continuation of the prudential isorrhope. If Luke and Matthew accept my recommendation, they will set their common chance-device so that, out of every 43 evenings over the long run, Luke will play the piano and Matthew refrain from trumpeting on 17 evenings, while Matthew will play the trumpet and Luke refrain from playing the piano on the remaining 26 evenings. The extent of the inroads they will make upon the co-operators' surplus by co-operating in this way is manifest in Diagram V.

I should not make this definitive recommendation to them until they had agreed upon the fairness and good sense of my provisional recommendation, when pairs of independent strategies were alone considered. This is because the Theory-of-Games argument for selecting the prudential isorrhope out of the beam of isorrhopes presupposes that the possible strategies of the two parties should be independent. When a coupled strategy is used the two parties are, from the standpoint of Theory of Games, conflated into one person, and the game ceases to be a two-person game.

35

So the argument for the fairness and good sense of my definitive recommendation consists of three stages:

(1) The von Neumann 'solution' for the competition for relative advantage has an outcome represented by the prudential isorrhope;

(2) The topmost point of this isorrhope is to be the outcome point when independent strategies are used;

(3) The point where this isorrhope (continued upwards, if necessary, as in our example) cuts the upper right-hand boundary of the total strategic region is to be the outcome point when (as in our example) it is advantageous to both parties to use a coupled strategy.

The argument for using the prudential isorrhope to determine the final outcome point is that this isorrhope yields what I believe both parties would agree to be an appropriate distribution of benefits in the region for which it is defined (the paired-strategies region where independent strategies are used), and there seems to me no good reason for departing from this principle of distribution when Luke and Matthew both increase their gains by agreeing together to use a coupled strategy.

My final recommendation for our example of a collaboration situation is, therefore, that Luke and Matthew should agree together that one or other (but not both) should play every evening, and that the playing time should be divided in the ratio 17 evenings for Luke to 26 evenings for Matthew. Whether they use a common chance-device to settle the division (as I have suggested) or prefer to do this in some other way will be a matter for their own convenience. They will be carrying out my recommendation if, one way or another, they manage on the average to share the playing time in the 17 to 26 ratio.

This arrangement is relatively advantageous to Matthew, and it is worth examining why this should be so. Matthew's advantage arises purely from the fact that Matthew, the trumpeter, prefers both of them playing at once to neither of them playing, whereas Luke, the pianist, prefers silence to cacophony. If the situation were reversed, with τ_{11} exchanging with τ_{22} in both their utility scales (the other alternatives retaining the same utilities), Diagram IV with the points T_{11} and T_{22} relabelled would then represent Luke's strategy lines and Diagram III Matthew's. The beam of isorrhopes would be unchanged; but the result of the isorrhopic competition will now be that the prudential isorrhope will be the one passing through the new T_{11}, i.e. it will be the lowest of the three drawn on Diagram V. The outcome point where this prudential isorrhope intersects the upper right-hand boundary $T_{21}T_{12}$ will be as far below the midpoint of this line as the outcome point of the original situation was above the midpoint; so the coupled strategy determined by the new outcome point will be that Luke should play 26 evenings to Matthew's 17. Exchanging T_{11} with T_{22} has exactly reversed the distribution of time between Luke and Matthew.

If both Luke and Matthew are indifferent between silence and cacophony, the points T_{11} and T_{22} will coalesce, and the prudential isorrhope, which passes through this common point, will intersect the line

$T_{21}T_{12}$ at its midpoint. So Luke and Matthew will divide the playing time equally, neither having an advantage over the other.

The fact that the original situation, represented by Diagrams III–V, is intrinsically advantageous to Matthew is represented on the diagrams by the geometrical fact that the range of the parabola touched by Matthew's strategy lines is more extensive than the range touched by Luke's. The angle through which Matthew can turn his selected strategy line, by choosing different probability combinations in which to mix his pure strategies, is greater than the angle through which Luke is able to turn his selected strategy line. Matthew has a greater degree of freedom than has Luke; if these degrees of freedom are measured in the simplest way, by assigning parameters to points on the parabola proportional to their distances, positive or negative, from the axis, the ratio of Matthew's to Luke's degree of freedom is as 26 to 17. Thus the division of playing time I recommend corresponds to a feature intrinsic to the logic of the situation. (In the example in which the points T_{11}, T_{22} coalesce, Luke's and Matthew's strategy lines will touch the parabola in exactly the same range of points.)

My recommendation as to how Luke and Matthew should maximize production while maintaining a fair distribution is, of course, not the only recommendation that can be made. Raiffa has formulated conditions which must be satisfied by any recommendation for it to be worth considering, but these conditions leave great latitude. Nash has proposed a general form of recommendation,[5] and I have tried out other general forms, all of which would give different results in our example. But my common-sense judgement of fairness is against all of them. So my recommendation has, I think, the negative virtue of being superior to the alternative recommendations that have been worked out. But I cannot expect Luke and Matthew to agree to it merely on that account.

Suppose that Luke, who comes off the worse in my recommendation, says to me that, though he is quite satisfied by the arguments for my recommendation *if* it is fair to take the isorrhopes as being lines parallel to the axis of the parabola, he is not satisfied as to the fairness of this premiss, upon which my whole argument rests. Why should he be prepared to agree that motion of an outcome point up a line parallel to the axis should be supposed to benefit both him and Matthew equally? What I have done, he will say, is to introduce surreptitiously, distracting attention by all my fine talk about parabolas, a *yardstick* for comparing his preference scale with that of Matthew, and this involves all the absurdities of Bentham's felicific calculus.

Luke is quite right in thinking that my choice of lines parallel to the parabola's axis as the isorrhopes is equivalent to an inter-personal comparison of utility scales. But the fairness of the distribution is concerned with its being equally fair to both parties, and nothing can be said about what it is to be equally fair to both parties in the situation in question without some method of comparing their preference scales for the alternatives in the situation. The cases of collaboration in which recommendations can be made which do not involve any inter-personal comparisons whatever are, as we have seen, those that are wholly non-competitive or those that are wholly competitive; and in both these cases the recommendation is how to behave sensibly or prudently rather than fairly. Fairness only comes in when the collaboration is neither wholly competitive nor wholly non-competitive; and it is here that some form of inter-personal comparison of utilities is unavoidable. If every such comparison is to be forbidden, the moral philosopher asked by Luke and Matthew to advise them in their particular predicament can do no more than repeat the platitude-paradox proclaimed by the pigs in George Orwell's *Animal Farm*: 'All animals are equal, but some animals are more equal than others'—a not very helpful remark. But one of the questions which I took it that Luke and Matthew were asking me was: 'Can you detect, and explain to us, any feature inherent in our situation which gives to one of us a natural advantage over the other; and, if so, can you attach to this natural advantage any number which we can use for fairly dividing our playing time?' Since the relevant features in the situation are solely their two preference scales, clearly there is nothing that can be said about the advantage which one may have over the other by having a different preference scale that does not involve an inter-personal comparison, by one means or another, of the two preference scales.

In proposing the axis of the parabola for settling

the directions of the isorrhopes, I am, it is true, making a comparison between Luke's and Matthew's preference scales, but one which is limited to the question of their fair collaboration in this particular example. I am not asserting that L-utilities should be related in this way to M-utilities for all purposes, but only for assessing the fairness of their shares in one particular common task. For this purpose my choice of isorrhopes has, it seems to me, outstanding merits in comparison with any other choice.

(1) If the isorrhopes are taken as parallel to the parabola's axis, each isorrhope will hit the parabola at one and only one point.[6] This will not in general be the case if the isorrhopes are taken as being straight lines in any other direction. Although I have discussed the collaboration situation in terms of a special example, I wish my recommendation to hold good in all cases in which the axis of the parabola slopes upwards from left to right; and if any other direction were specified in general for the isorrhopic beam, there would be cases in which the prudential isorrhope would fall into two separate parts, each part hitting the parabola at one point. This would seriously complicate the argument for any recommendation based upon the intersection of the prudential isorrhope with the parabola.

(2) The direction of the axis of the parabola is also the direction of the line joining the midpoints of the pairs of base points which are not joined by any strategy line (i.e. the line joining the midpoint of $T_{11}T_{22}$ to the midpoint of $T_{21}T_{12}$). Thus the isorrhopes, and the final recommendation which is in

terms of the intersection of the prudential isorrhope with the boundary of the total strategic region, can be explained without any reference to a parabola at all. (This will be particularly convenient for the cases in which the four line segments which represent the four pure strategies form a convex quadrilateral.) There is a somewhat sophisticated sense of 'symmetry' in which the pure strategy lines may be said to lie symmetrically about the line joining the midpoints of $T_{11}T_{22}$ and of $T_{21}T_{12}$, and this symmetry may, to some people, be intuitively obvious as a criterion for fairness.[7]

(3) Any line parallel to the axis of a parabola bisects all the chords of the parabola joining pairs of points where the two tangents from a point on this line touch the parabola. If isorrhopes are taken as parallel to the parabola's axis, the isorrhope passing through the point O where the vertical and horizontal tangents to the parabola intersect will, when continued inside the parabola, bisect the chord joining the points V and H where these tangents touch the parabola, and thus the slope of the beam of isorrhopes will be given by the ratio of the length of OV to that of OH (see Diagram VI, p. 43).

This ratio has an important interpretation. The vertical tangent of which OV is a part represents the von Neumann prudential strategy for Luke; if Luke employs this strategy, the outcome point will lie on this tangent and consequently Luke will secure an L-utility represented by its x co-ordinate whatever strategy Matthew may employ. Similarly, the horizontal tangent of which OH is a part is the prudential strategy for Matthew. But, in our example, the horizontal tangent is also one of the possible strategy lines for Luke to choose; if Luke uses the strategy represented by the horizontal tangent, the outcome point will lie on this tangent and consequently Luke will ensure that Matthew will

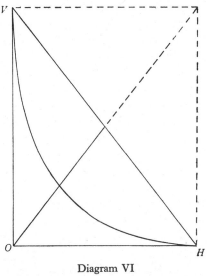

Diagram VI

secure an M-utility represented by the y co-ordinate of this tangent, whatever strategy Matthew himself may employ. Luke, that is, by using his *counter-prudential strategy* (as I shall call it) will compel Matthew to obtain what Matthew would get by himself acting prudentially, whether Matthew wants this result or not. Similarly, Matthew, by using his counter-prudential strategy represented by his taking the vertical tangent as strategy line, will ensure that Luke obtains no more and no less than what Luke himself would get by acting prudentially.

Consider now what are the outcome points resulting from the four conjunctions of Luke's prudential and counter-prudential strategies with Matthew's prudential and counter-prudential strategies, remembering that the choice by both of the same tangent to the parabola as strategy line yields as outcome point the point where this tangent touches the parabola. The outcome point will be O, the intersection of the vertical and horizontal tangents, if either both act prudentially or both act counter-prudentially. But the outcome point will be V, the point of contact of the vertical tangent, if Luke acts prudentially but Matthew counter-prudentially, and it will be H, the point of contact of the horizontal tangent, if Matthew acts prudentially but Luke counter-prudentially. Thus each will gain by transferring from a prudential strategy to a counter-prudential strategy while the other keeps to a prudential strategy, and the lengths OV and OH represent the increments of M-utility or of L-utility which Matthew and Luke respectively will gain in this way.

The choice of the direction of the parabola's axis for the direction of the isorrhopic beam is thus equivalent to agreeing to compare Luke's and Matthew's utility scales by taking the increment in the former represented by the length of OH as being on a parity with the increment in the latter represented by the length of OV. To put the matter in another way, it corresponds to taking the lengths of OH and OV as representing the natural units of the L-utility scale and of the M-utility scale respectively, these natural units being imposed by the logic of the collaboration situation, and of agreeing to equate these units for the purpose of determining the fairness of a recommendation. That there is a perfectly good sense in which these units are naturally imposed by the situation is shown by the fact that the parabola could have been uniquely specified in a way alternative to the three ways already used; namely, as being the parabola touching a specified vertical line OV at a specified point V and a specified horizontal line OH at a specified point H.[8] To treat the L-utility natural unit as equivalent in fairness to the M-utility natural unit is to agree that, there being no other satisfactory criterion for inter-personal fairness, each collaborator should be regarded as benefiting equally by a change from a prudential to a counter-prudential strategy when his colleague is holding to his prudential strategy.

This, in fact, was the first criterion for inter-personal fairness which I came upon when I started working on the subject. Why I have not put it at the forefront of my exposition is that it is only in some of the possible cases of the general collaboration situation that the lines either of Luke's strategy scroll or of Matthew's strategy scroll include both the vertical and the horizontal tangents. To apply this criterion in general would therefore require treating all the cases differing in this way from those exemplified by our example as being cases resembling the example in all relevant respects except that the possible strategy lines were subject to a severer restriction. This restriction, however, would have to be considered as not affecting the fairness of treating the natural utility units as equivalent. I think that such an argument is a perfectly sound one; but I find it less convincing than that based upon the direction of the parabola's axis, which is straightforwardly applicable to all the cases.

The principle of equating natural utility units enables me directly to connect my treatment of the problem with that given by Raiffa for situations in which the utility scales of the two collaborators can be measured in terms of a common unit (e.g. a monetary unit) so that it makes sense to speak of the *difference* between a utility of Luke's and one of Matthew's. For this situation Raiffa proposes that the two parties should first solve their zero-sum 'non-co-operative relative game' (in which the outcomes are the differences between the utilities yielded to Luke and to Matthew by the outcomes of the collaboration situation), and then improve on this solution by advancing to the upper right-hand boundary of their total strategic region by a route which yields equal increments of utility to each party.[9] This corresponds exactly to my method of selecting the prudential isorrhope, and then of advancing up this isorrhope to the boundary (and I owe the method to Raiffa's paper, though I justify it, and therefore expound it, somewhat differently). Raiffa, however, did not see any way of dealing with situations in which the utility scales were not expressible in terms of a common unit; here my idea of a natural utility unit, imposed upon the two parties by the logic of the collaboration situation, which also makes it plausible to equate these units for the purpose of making a recommendation, is complementary to Raiffa's idea as to how to treat a collaboration situation in which common units are given from the beginning.

Determining fairness by equating the natural utility units seems to be the best way of passing to those cases in which the axis of the parabola, instead of sloping upwards, slopes downwards from left to right. Diagram VII (p. 48) shows an example of such a case, in which Luke's preference scale is exactly the reverse of what it was in Diagrams III–V, while Matthew's preference scale remains exactly the same. The quadrilateral of pure strategies and the parabola determined by them of Diagram VII thus form the reflexion in a vertical mirror of the pure strategy quadrilateral and its related parabola of Diagram V. Since the axis of the new parabola slopes downwards, the movement of an outcome point in a direction parallel to it would increase Luke's utility while diminishing Matthew's, or vice versa: so this direction cannot be taken as settling the direction for the new isorrhopic beam. But the natural units of L-utility and of M-utility are unaltered by the reflexion; what is changed is that Luke will now lose one natural unit of L-utility instead of gaining one such unit by transferring from a prudential to a counter-prudential strategy while Matthew holds on to his prudential strategy. Thus the direction of the new isorrhopic beam can be taken to be the same as that of the old isorrhopic

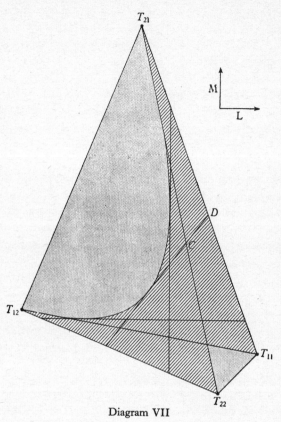

Diagram VII

beam; unlike the other features of the situation, it is unchanged by reflexion. My recommendation for the cases in which the axis of the parabola slopes downwards will thus be based upon taking as isorrhopes lines sloping upwards from left to right whose upward slope is equal to the downward slope of the parabola's axis.

Taking this direction for the isorrhopes in the example represented by Diagram VII will lead to a recommendation which is interestingly different from my recommendation for the example of Diagrams III–V. The prudential isorrhope resulting from the isorrhopic competition between Luke and Matthew, which is of the second type (p. 17), is the unique isorrhope which is a tangent to the parabola; it coincides both with one of Luke's strategy lines and with one of Matthew's strategy lines. Thus the condition that the outcome point should lie on the prudential isorrhope can be satisfied by either Luke or Matthew or both choosing the prudential isorrhope as his strategy line. If Matthew makes this choice, Luke can then maximize both their utilities by choosing $T_{21}T_{22}$ as his strategy line; the outcome point will be the point marked C on Diagram VII. If Luke chooses the prudential isorrhope as his strategy line, Matthew can then maximize both their utilities by choosing $T_{21}T_{11}$ as his strategy line; since the outcome point D resulting therefrom will be preferred by both of them to the lower point C, my recommendation will be that they should follow this latter course, which will result in Matthew playing the trumpet every evening and Luke playing the piano on the average 23 evenings out of 40. The requirement of maximum production subject to fair distribution will here be satisfied by a division of labour, by Matthew taking over the maximizing of production while Luke concerns himself with seeing that the products are distributed fairly. The mixed strategy of Luke's which effects this is equivalent to the half-and-half probability combination of his prudential and of his counter-prudential mixed strategies; so the way in which Luke should behave is to act prudently in his own interest half the time and prudently in Matthew's interest the other half of the time, Matthew being completely occupied with production. If he tries to cheat Matthew by neglecting to act as much in Matthew's interest as in his own, Matthew can retort by changing to that strategy of his which yields the prudential isorrhope, and thus taking over the job of distribution. Since Luke would certainly lose by Matthew's doing this he will not be tempted to cheat. Matthew, on the other hand, will be kept to the highest production by the fact that he will suffer as much as Luke if he diminishes it. In the language of the *Republic*, Matthew will be the Worker and Luke the Guardian; but this will not be unjust to the Worker, since he will be allowed to take over the Guardian's functions whenever he is dissatisfied with the way in which the Guardian is performing them—a possibility not envisaged by Plato.

Let us now ascend the ivory tower of ethical analysis to get some view of the logical geography of our discussion. The context is a *consultation*; Luke and Matthew are supposed to have come to consult me as to how they should act in a specific collaboration situation in which they find themselves. I tell them that I cannot give them any advice unless they provide me with the relevant data, which is sufficient information about their preferences for the alternative possible outcomes of the collaboration, and for probability combinations of these alternative outcomes, to enable me to measure, in the weak sense, each of their preference scales separately. In our discussion I have assumed that they are able to provide me with this information. I then do some simple mathematical calculations, as a result of which I make a specific recommendation to them as to how to act, the nature of the recommendation I make depending upon into which of three kinds falls the collaboration situation. After I have made my recommendation, I shall apply certain complimentary adjectives to the course of action I recommend.

If the situation is a wholly competitive one, I shall remark that no behaviour not in accordance with my recommendation would seem to me to be *prudent* for either of them in that situation.

In this kind of case I should make the same recommendation and the same remark if Luke or Matthew came to consult me by himself (provided, of course, that he could provide me with the relevant data about both their preferences), since I could not improve upon my recommendation if they were willing to agree together how to act.

But if the collaboration situation is one which is not a wholly competitive one, I shall insist on making my recommendation to Luke and Matthew jointly, since my recommendation for this kind of case is that they should *co-operate* in a specific way. And I shall emphasize my recommendation by remarking, if the situation is wholly non-competitive, that no other behaviour would seem to me to be *sensible*, or, if the situation is partly (but only partly) competitive, that no other behaviour would seem to me to be *sensible, prudent and fair*, for the two of them together in the situation in which they find themselves in which they can both profit by co-operation.

In all these cases I shall not apply the complimentary epithets until after I have made the recommendations and given my reasons for making them. My third recommendation, for example, I shall justify by an argument employing a comparison of Luke's preference scale with Matthew's in a particular way, the reasons for proposing this particular way of inter-personal comparison being concerned with the formal analogy I have discovered between the logic of the collaboration situation and the geometry of a parabola. It is true that, after calculating what recommendation to make on the basis of this geometrical analogy, I examined the behaviour recommended, and the behaviour that would be recommended in other cases, to see if it would offend common sense to call it sensible, prudent and fair, and decided that it would not so offend. But I did not start with a precise notion of what it would be like for a collaboration to be sensible, prudent and fair, and deduce therefrom my recommendation that Luke and Matthew should divide their playing time in the ratio of 17 to 26.

What I have been doing is what some philosophers would describe as giving an 'explication' or a 'rational reconstruction' of the concept *sensible-prudent-and-fair* as applied in collaboration situations, where a concept, used loosely by common sense, is tightened up by an exact criterion being given as to the circumstances under which it should be applied. Another way to describe my line of thought is in terms of the comparison drawn by John Wisdom between what he calls 'unconventional reflection', reflection 'in which it is necessary to introduce a new notation or remould an old one in order to express that new awareness of the known which this reflection brings', and legal discussion of the applicability of a legal term such as 'negligence' to a specific case.[10] Like the lawyer I am neither ascertaining new facts about Luke's and Matthew's collaboration situation—all the relevant facts became known to me when I was given sufficient data to calculate the two preference scales—nor am I merely talking about the use of the adjectives 'sensible', 'prudent', 'fair', either the customary use or a proposed new use. What I have done has been to adduce intellectual considerations to enable *me* to make a practical decision—the practical decision as to how to advise Luke and Matthew when they ask me how they should collaborate.

The resemblance of the 'solutions' of generalized two-person games to judicial decisions has been noticed by Raiffa, who, 'motivated [as he says] by the role of arbitration in collective bargaining disputes', calls them *arbitration schemes*.[11] 'Arbitration' seemed too pretentious a term to apply to the advice I should give to Luke and Matthew as to how to settle their musical dispute; and since I should not announce my recommendation to them without accompanying it by my grounds for making it, I

53

should hope that the sweet reasonableness of my parabolas would make our meeting one for 'conciliation' rather than for 'arbitration' within the meaning of Industrial Disputes Acts. But if Luke and Matthew are more concerned with obtaining a definite decision than with being convinced of its justice, and, having discovered that the Knightbridge Chair was originally the Professorship of Moral Theology and Casuistical Divinity, demand of me as the University's professional casuist that I should pass judgement upon their moral problem, arbitration will be the *mot juste* for my award of the 17 evenings in 43 to Luke and the 26 to Matthew.

In expounding to you my reasons for this award I have made a small contribution towards realizing Condorcet's dream *éclairer les Sciences morales et politiques par le flambeau de l'Algèbre*.[12] The algebra I enlist for this purpose is the new mathematical Theory of Games; and I hope, by showing how it can yield results, to encourage others as well as myself to pursue and apply it further. And if anyone is inclined to doubt whether any serious enlightenment can come from the discreetly shaded candles of the card-room, I would remind him that, three hundred years ago this year (1954), that most serious of men, Blaise Pascal, laid the foundations of the mathematical theory of probability in a correspondence with Fermat about a question asked him by the Chevalier de Méré, who had found that he was losing at a game of dice more often than he had expected. No one today will doubt the intensity, though he may dislike the colour, of the (shall I say)

54

sodium light cast by statistical mathematics, direct descendant of theory of games of chance, upon the social sciences. Perhaps in another three hundred years' time economic and political and other branches of moral philosophy will bask in radiation from a source—theory of games of strategy—whose prototype was kindled round the poker tables of Princeton.

NOTES

1 (p. 6) Henry Sidgwick, *The Methods of Ethics* (6th ed., London, 1901), pp. xxxiv, 416f.

2 (p. 7) The extension to the $n \times n$ case is given in Appendix, §2.

3 (p. 21) The references are to Howard Raiffa, in *Contributions to the Theory of Games*, vol. 2, edited by H. W. Kuhn and A. W. Tucker (Annals of Mathematics Studies, no. 28; Princeton, 1953), pp. 361–87; John Nash, in *Econometrica*, vol. 21 (1953), pp. 128–40 (see also *Econometrica*, vol. 18 (1950), pp. 155–62; vol. 21 (1953), pp. 141–54).

4 (p. 26) Points equidistantly spaced along a line u are in a one-one algebraic correspondence (a projectivity, a homography) with points equidistantly spaced along a line v; so, if u and v lie in the same plane, the lines joining corresponding points on u and on v envelope a conic. Since the point at infinity on u corresponds to the point at infinity on v, the line at infinity in the plane touches the conic, which is therefore a parabola. The line u is the line which joins the intersection of u and v to the point on u corresponding to this intersection, regarded as a point on v; so u touches the parabola. Similarly, v touches the parabola. (If any two corresponding points coincide, the parabola degenerates.) Since a conic is uniquely determined by any five of its tangents, a parabola (a conic touching the line at infinity) is uniquely determined by four tangents.

5 (p. 39) John Nash, 'Two-person co-operative games', *Econometrica*, vol. 21 (1953), pp. 128–40. Nash's most ingenious argument, which applies to the most general case, is couched in quite different language from mine. In my language, and for the example of Diagrams III–V, it is equivalent to taking for the direction of the isorrhopic beam a slope which is the negative (i.e. the reflexion in a vertical or in a horizontal mirror) of the slope of the line $T_{21}T_{12}$, the upper right-hand boundary of the total strategic region. The beam of isorrhopes being thus determined, Nash's method for selecting the prudential isorrhope (by the solution of a 'threat game') is similar to mine, and yields in our example the isorrhope passing through T_{11}. Thus Nash's procedure for our example would be to draw the line through T_{11} whose upward slope is equal to the downward slope of $T_{21}T_{12}$, and to recommend a coupled strategy which would yield the intersection of these two lines as outcome point. This would work out at dividing the playing time in the ratio of 1 for Luke to 13 for Matthew. If the base point T_{21} were to be moved slightly to the right (as in the case, for instance, in which the L-utility differences stood in the ratios 1 to $2\frac{1}{2}$ to $2\frac{1}{2}$ instead of 1 to 2 to 3), Matthew would play every evening and Luke never. These recommendations seem to me clearly unfair on Luke.

6 (p. 41) The axis of a parabola passes through the point W on the line at infinity where this line touches the parabola. Every line parallel to the axis (every *diameter* of the parabola) also passes through W and intersects the parabola at one other point.

7 (p. 42) The centres of all the conics touching four fixed lines are collinear. If these lines are the four pure strategy lines, one of these conics is the parabola determined by the four lines, with centre at W, a

8 57 B

second is the point-pair T_{11}, T_{22}, with centre at the midpoint of $T_{11}T_{22}$, a third is the point-pair T_{21}, T_{12}, with centre at the midpoint of $T_{21}T_{12}$. Thus the line w joining these two midpoints passes through W and so is a diameter of the parabola. If P and Q are any points on $T_{11}T_{21}$ and $T_{22}T_{12}$ respectively such that $T_{11}P/PT_{21} = T_{22}Q/QT_{12}$, PQ will be bisected by w.

8 (p. 45) A conic is uniquely determined by three of its tangents together with the points of contact of two of them. So a parabola is uniquely determined by two tangents and their points of contact.

9 (p. 46) Howard Raiffa, loc. cit., pp. 377 ff.

10 (p. 53) John Wisdom, *Philosophy and Psycho-Analysis* (Oxford, 1953), pp. 249 ff. The phrase I have quoted about 'unconventional reflection' occurs on p. 253.

11 (p. 53) Howard Raiffa, loc. cit., p. 361. The title of his paper is 'Arbitration schemes for generalized two-person games'.

12 (p. 54) J. Bertrand's phrase about Condorcet, in *Calcul des Probabilités* (Paris, 1889), p. xviii. In *Tableau Général de la Science, qui a pour objet l'application du calcul aux sciences morales et politiques* (1795) Condorcet wrote: 'Plusieurs questions de jurisprudence ne peuvent être résolues sans emprunter le secours du calcul.... Tel serait le partage, soit d'une obligation qu'on doit remplir en commun, soit d'une chose à laquelle divers individus ont des droits, toutes les fois que ces droits sont mêlés de considérations éventuelles qui nécessitent le recours au calcul des probabilités, ou qu'ils nécessitent des évaluations pour lesquelles ce calcul ou la théorie des valeurs moyennes sont indispensables' (*Œuvres*, éd. Arago, t. 1 (Paris, 1847–9), p. 571).

APPENDIX

ALGEBRAIC TREATMENT OF A GENERAL TWO-PERSON COLLABORATION SITUATION

1. 2×2 *collaboration situations*

1·1. Introduce the notion of *weighted strategy* explained as follows:

Let w be any number, positive, negative or zero. A weighted strategy $L(w)$ for L is to be obtained by combining L's pure strategy L_1, weighted with a weight-factor of $(1-w)$, with L's pure strategy L_2, weighted with a weight factor of w, in such a way that the L-utility resulting from the use by L of $L(w)$ is equal to the L-utility that would result from the use by L of L_1, multiplied by the factor $(1-w)$, added to the L-utility that would result from the use by L of L_2, multiplied by the factor w, for every strategy used by M.

If $0 < w < 1$, $L(w)$ is the mixed strategy obtained by combining L_1 with a probability of $(1-w)$ with L_2 with a probability of w. If $w = 0$, $L(w)$ is the pure strategy L_1; if $w = 1$, $L(w)$ is the pure strategy L_2.

A weighted strategy $M(w)$ for M is to be similarly explained as one obtained by similarly combining M's pure strategy M_1, weighted with a weight-factor of $(1-w)$, with M's pure strategy M_2, weighted with a weight-factor of w.

A *weight* w may be regarded as similar to a *mixing probability* p except that it is not restricted by the condition $0 \leqslant p \leqslant 1$; and a weighted strategy may be regarded as similar to a mixed strategy except that it is not subject to the boundary conditions imposed by the positions of the pure strategies. Every mixing probability is a weight; and every strategy, mixed or pure, is a weighted strategy. Many weighted strategies, however, will be unrealizable as actual strategies.

Use of the set of weighted strategies as an extension of the set of actually realizable strategies, corresponding to the use of weight as an extension of mixing probability, enables the algebra to be stated in a form which avoids inequalities, the idea for which I owe to Irving Kaplansky's early treatment of 'completely mixed' zero-sum two-person games (*Annals of Mathematics*, vol. 46 (1945), pp. 474–9).

Weights, like mixing probabilities, are invariant with respect to linear transformations of the utilities concerned.

1·2. Let the two utility scales for the four possible outcomes obtainable by conjoining one of L's two pure strategies L_1, L_2 with one of M's two pure strategies M_1, M_2 be represented by

	L-utility table (values of x)			M-utility table (values of y)	
	M_1	M_2		M_1	M_2
L_1	a_{11}	a_{12}	L_1	b_{11}	b_{12}
L_2	a_{21}	a_{22}	L_2	b_{21}	b_{22}

Any significant result must be invariant with respect to any linear transformation of the L-utilities $x' = u_1 x + u_2$ and to any linear transformation of the M-utilities $y' = v_1 y + v_2$, with $u_1 > 0$, $v_1 > 0$. Such linear transformations will be called *utility transformations*. Utility transformations form a group.

To avoid, in the first instance, exceptional cases suppose that

$$g = a_{11} - a_{12} - a_{21} + a_{22} \neq 0, \quad h = b_{11} - b_{12} - b_{21} + b_{22} \neq 0.$$

Then
$$c = \frac{1}{g}(a_{11} - a_{12}), \quad d = \frac{1}{h}(b_{11} - b_{12}),$$

$$e = \frac{1}{g}(a_{11} - a_{21}), \quad f = \frac{1}{h}(b_{11} - b_{21}),$$

are the solutions respectively of the equations

$$a_{11}(1 - c) + a_{21}c = a_{12}(1 - c) + a_{22}c,$$
$$b_{11}(1 - d) + b_{21}d = b_{12}(1 - d) + b_{22}d,$$
$$a_{11}(1 - e) + a_{12}e = a_{21}(1 - e) + a_{22}e,$$
$$b_{11}(1 - f) + b_{12}f = b_{21}(1 - f) + b_{22}f.$$

c, d, e, f are all invariant with respect to linear transformations of the utilities concerned.

Consider L's weighted strategies $L(c)$, $L(d)$, and M's weighted strategies $M(e)$, $M(f)$.

The utilities resulting from the use by L of a weighted strategy $L(u)$ and by M of a weighted strategy $M(v)$ are linear functions of u and linear functions of v. Hence, since use of $L(c)$ yields an L-utility of $a_{11}(1 - c) + a_{21}c$ if M_1 is used and of $a_{12}(1 - c) + a_{22}c$ if M_2 is used, the L-utility resulting from the use by L of $L(c)$ will be constant whatever weighted strategy is used by M, with a constant value $a_0 = \frac{1}{g}(a_{11}a_{22} - a_{12}a_{21})$. And the L-utility resulting from the use by M of $M(e)$ will be constant whatever weighted strategy is used by L; this constant value is also a_0. Similarly, the M-utility resulting from the use either by L of $L(d)$ or by M of $M(f)$ will be $b_0 = \frac{1}{h}(b_{11}b_{22} - b_{12}b_{21})$, whatever weighted strategy is used by the other party. If L uses L(c) and M uses M(e), the resulting M-utility will be

$$b_{11} + h(ce - cf - de) = b_0 + hk,$$

where $k = (c-d)(e-f)$. If L uses L(d) and M uses M(f), the resulting L-utility will be

$$a_{11} + g(df - cf - de) = a_0 + gk.$$

If the pair of utility tables are infinitely expanded so that every weighted strategy of L is represented by a row and every weighted strategy of M by a column, there will be exactly one row in each table, the row in the first representing L(c) and that in the second L(d), and exactly one column in each table, the column in the first representing M(e) and that in the second M(f), in which the utilities are equal along the row or down the column respectively. These four weighted strategies will be called the *equalizing strategies*, and their weights c, d, e, f the *equalizing weights*, for the collaboration situation. L(c) and L(d) will be *row-equalizing*, M(e) and M(f) will be *column-equalizing*; L(c) and M(e) will be L-*utility-equalizing*, L(d) and M(f) will be M-*utility-equalizing*. If $c = d$, the two row-equalizing strategies coalesce; if $e = f$, the two column-equalizing strategies coalesce. If both $c = d$ and $e = f$ so that the four equalizing strategies reduce to two by a double coalescence, the collaboration situation (if $h/g < 0$) reduces to the wholly competitive case treated by von Neumann, whose 'solution' (if it is of the second type, where the equalizing weights are mixing probabilities) is the pair of equalizing strategies, one for L, one for M. These yield an L-utility for L of a_0 and an M-utility for M of b_0.

Suppose now that $c \neq d$ and $e \neq f$, i.e.

$$k = (c-d)(e-f) \neq 0.$$

The equalizing strategies will then be represented by

two distinct rows and two distinct columns. If these two rows and two columns are extracted from the infinitely expanded utility tables, their overlaps will form a pair of four-square subtables (the *cores* of the expanded tables):

	L-utility core (values of x)			M-utility core (values of y)	
	M(e)	M(f)		M(e)	M(f)
L(c)	a_0	a_0	L(c)	b_0+hk	b_0
L(d)	a_0	a_0+gk	L(d)	b_0	b_0

According to the argument of pp. 42 ff. the absolute values of gk and of hk may be taken as 'natural units' of L-utility (x) and of M-utility (y) respectively. The utility transformations $x' = \dfrac{1}{|g|}x$, $y' = \dfrac{1}{|h|}y$ will transform the utility tables expressed in terms of x and y respectively into *reduced* tables expressed in terms of x' and y' in which the natural units are both $|k|$.

The relative advantage of L over M for each possible outcome may then be specified as the difference between the reduced L- and M-utilities $x' - y'$. The relative advantage of M over L will be $y' - x'$; so the competition for relative advantage will be a zero-sum game between L and M, a 'relative game' of the sort discussed by Raiffa (loc. cit., pp. 377 ff.).

1·3. Any of the four equalizing weights lying between 0 and 1 inclusive will be a mixing probability and the corresponding equalizing strategy will be a mixed (or pure) strategy with that mixing probability.

If

$0 \leqslant c \leqslant 1$, L(c) will be L's prudential strategy;

if $0 \leqslant d \leqslant 1$, L(d) will be L's counter-prudential strategy;

if $0 \leqslant e \leqslant 1$, M(e) will be M's counter-prudential strategy;

if $0 \leqslant f \leqslant 1$, M(f) will be M's prudential strategy.

For the principal example of a general collaboration situation used in the lecture (represented by Diagrams III–V), the two utility scales may be expressed as

<table>
<tr><td colspan="3">L-utility table
(values of x)</td><td colspan="3">M-utility table
(values of y)</td></tr>
<tr><td></td><td>M_1</td><td>M_2</td><td></td><td>M_1</td><td>M_2</td></tr>
<tr><td>L_1</td><td>100</td><td>700</td><td>L_1</td><td>200</td><td>300</td></tr>
<tr><td>L_2</td><td>400</td><td>200</td><td>L_2</td><td>1000</td><td>100</td></tr>
</table>

Here

$$g = -800, \quad h = -1000, \quad h/g = 5/4; \quad a_0 = 325, \quad b_0 = 280;$$
$$c = \tfrac{3}{4}, \quad d = \tfrac{1}{10}, \quad e = \tfrac{3}{8}, \quad f = \tfrac{4}{5}, \quad k = -\tfrac{221}{800}.$$

Since the equalizing weights c, d, e, f are all proper fractions, they are all mixing probabilities for the equalizing mixed strategies. The utility tables expanded to include these strategies and arranged so that the weightings increase downwards along each column and rightwards along each row are shown on pp. 66–7. The numbers in the left-hand and upper borders are the mixing probabilities for the rows and the columns respectively (i.e. the weights c, d, e, f, 0, 1). The numbers in the right-hand and lower borders are the parabolic parameters which will appear in §1·4; they have been obtained by rescaling each set of mixing probabilities so that -1 corresponds to c and to e and 1 to d and to f. The centrally situated four-square subtables form the cores of the tables.

1·4. *The parabolas.* Suppose, as before, that

$$g \neq 0, \quad h \neq 0, \quad k \neq 0.$$

Consider the parabola P given in rectangular Cartesian co-ordinates by the equation

$$\left(\frac{x-x_0}{gk} - \frac{y-y_0}{hk}\right)^2 - 2\left(\frac{x-x_0}{gk} + \frac{y-y_0}{hk}\right) + 1 = 0.$$

P is the parabola which touches the horizontal line $y = y_0$ at $x = x_0 + gk$ and the vertical line $x = x_0$ at $y = y_0 + hk$. The slope $(\mathrm{d}y/\mathrm{d}x)$ of the axis of P is h/g. The axis slopes upwards if g and h are of the same sign; it slopes downwards if g and h differ in sign. P lies in the upper right-hand quadrant, in the lower left-hand quadrant, in the upper left-hand quadrant or in the lower right-hand quadrant of the Cartesian plane, according as gk and hk are both positive, both negative, gk negative and hk positive, gk positive and hk negative, respectively.

The parabola P may equally well be specified in the same co-ordinate system by the pair of equations in terms of a *parabolic parameter* t:

$$x = x_0 + \tfrac{1}{4}gk(1+t)^2, \quad y = y_0 + \tfrac{1}{4}hk(1-t)^2.$$

Here $t = 1$ yields P's point of contact with its horizontal tangent $y = y_0$, and $t = -1$ yields P's point of contact with its vertical tangent $x = x_0$. $t = 0$ yields the point on P where the line through (x_0, y_0) parallel to P's axis (the diameter of P through (x_0, y_0)) intersects P, and the value of t for any point on P is proportional to the distance of the point from this diameter.

The transformation

$$x = x_0 + \tfrac{1}{4}gk(1+\lambda)(1+\mu),$$
$$y = y_0 + \tfrac{1}{4}hk(1-\lambda)(1-\mu)$$

L-utility table
(values of x)

		M_1	$M(e)$	$M(f)$	M_2	
	w	0	$\frac{3}{8}$	$\frac{4}{5}$	1	
L_1	0	100	325	580	700	$1\frac{4}{13}$
$L(d)$	$\frac{1}{10}$	130	325	546	650	1
$L(c)$	$\frac{3}{4}$	325	325	325	325	-1
L_2	1	400	325	240	200	$-1\frac{10}{13}$
		$-2\frac{13}{17}$	-1	1	$1\frac{16}{17}$	t

effects a one-one correspondence between unordered pairs $[\lambda, \mu]$ of values of the parabolic parameter t and points (x, y) of the plane which lie on or outside the parabola.

If λ is restricted to the closed interval I from $\frac{c+d}{c-d}$ to $\frac{c+d-2}{c-d}$ inclusive, and μ is restricted to the closed interval J from $\frac{e+f}{e-f}$ to $\frac{e+f-2}{e-f}$ inclusive, the corresponding point (x, y) is confined to the paired-strategies region, and vice versa. L's choice of a strategy is equivalent to

M-utility table
(values of y)

	w	M_1	$M(e)$	$M(f)$	M_2	
		0	$\frac{3}{8}$	$\frac{4}{5}$	1	
L_1	0	200	$237\frac{1}{2}$	280	300	$1\frac{4}{13}$
$L(d)$	$\frac{1}{10}$	280	280	280	280	1
$L(c)$	$\frac{3}{4}$	800	$556\frac{1}{4}$	280	150	-1
L_2	1	1000	$662\frac{1}{2}$	280	100	$-1\frac{10}{13}$
		$-2\frac{13}{17}$	-1	1	$1\frac{16}{17}$	t

a choice of a value of λ lying in I, M's choice of a strategy is equivalent to a choice of a value of μ lying in $\mathcal{J}$. Choice of a pure strategy is equivalent to choice of an end-point of I or of $\mathcal{J}$ respectively. A choice by L of a value of λ lying outside I or by M of a value of μ lying outside $\mathcal{J}$ will correspond to a choice of an unrealizable weighted strategy.

For λ fixed at λ_0, the transformation

$$x = x_0 + \tfrac{1}{4}gk(1+\lambda_0)\,(1+\mu),$$
$$y = y_0 + \tfrac{1}{4}hk(1-\lambda_0)\,(1-\mu)$$

effects a one-one correspondence between values of μ

and points (x, y) on the tangent to P at the point on it whose parabolic parameter is λ_0. Thus the tangent at $t = \lambda_0$ is the locus of outcome points obtainable by M choosing any value for μ when L chooses λ_0. Similarly, for μ fixed at μ_0, the tangent at $t = \mu_0$ is the locus of outcome points obtainable by L choosing any value for λ when M chooses μ_0. The intersection of these two tangents (the λ_0 *strategy line* and the μ_0 *strategy line*) is the outcome point obtainable if L chooses λ_0 and M chooses μ_0; if $\lambda_0 = \mu_0$ the two strategy lines coalesce into one, and the outcome point is its point of contact with the parabola P.

The vertical tangent to P (at $t = -1$) represents L's prudential strategy if L can realize it as a strategy line, and M's counter-prudential strategy if M can realize it as a strategy line. The horizontal tangent to P (at $t = 1$) represents, if realizable, L's counter-prudential and M's prudential strategy. The vertical and horizontal tangents will represent the weighted strategies $L(c)$, $L(d)$ respectively for L, and $M(e)$, $M(f)$ respectively for M, whether or not these weighted strategies are realizable.

If reduced co-ordinates x', y', given by $x' = \dfrac{1}{|g|} x$, $y' = \dfrac{1}{|h|} y$, are used, the reduced parabola in the x', y' plane has the slope of its axis either 1 or -1. According to the argument of the lecture the direction of the isorrhopic beam in this plane will then be fixed at 1 in all cases. This is equivalent to playing Raiffa's zero-sum 'relative game'.

1·5. *Exceptional cases*. Consider first the exceptional cases obtained by permitting $k = (c - d)(e - f) = 0$.

If $k = 0$, the parabola-scroll degenerates into two pencils of lines, the pencil of lines through the point (x_0, y_0) and the pencil of parallel lines of slope h/g (i.e. the pencil of lines through the point on the line at infinity in the direction h/g). The line through (x_0, y_0) with slope h/g will be the axis of this degenerate parabola-scroll.

If $c=d$ and $e \neq f$, L's strategy lines will all be parallel with slope h/g and M's strategy lines will all pass through (x_0, y_0). And vice versa if $c \neq d$ and $e=f$. In these cases the method of the lecture can be employed by taking the direction of the isorrhopic beam as being $|h/g|$.

If both $c=d$ and $e=f$, all the strategy lines both of L and of M are segments of the line through (x_0, y_0) with slope h/g. If $h/g<0$ the collaboration situation is a wholly competitive one; and its 'solution', if it is of the second wholly competitive type, is given by the point (x_0, y_0). The fact that the total strategic region is in this case a straight line makes the direction of the isorrhopes irrelevant to settling the solution; hence in this case no inter-personal comparison of utilities is required at any stage in the argument.

Next consider the exceptional cases in which $g=0$ while $h \neq 0$.

Unless all the four a's are equal, the strategy lines envelope a proper parabola whose axis is vertical. If the direction of the isorrhopic beam is taken as vertical, which considerations of continuity would suggest, the isorrhopic competition will result in the prudential isorrhope being the vertical line passing through the outcome point which would result from both L and M using prudential strategies in the wholly competitive situation (which is of the first type) in which L aims at maximizing, and M at minimizing, L's utility. A recommendation based upon this prudential isorrhope seems a fair one (in the cases which are not wholly non-competitive), though it might be preferable to take the isorrhopic beam as making a very small angle with the vertical so as to give L some motive for co-operation. (If the four a's are equal, the parabola-scroll with a vertical axis degenerates into two pencils of lines through two points on this axis, one at infinity.)

The exceptional cases in which $h = 0$ while $g \neq 0$, where the parabola has a horizontal axis, can be treated similarly.

If both $g = 0$ and $h = 0$, the parabola-scroll degenerates into two pencils of lines through two points on the line at infinity, the L-strategy lines being all parallel and the M-strategy lines all parallel. Since the axis of the degenerate parabola-scroll is the line at infinity, which has every direction, there is no possibility of using this direction to settle that of the isorrhopic beam, and no inter-personal comparison of utilities is naturally given. However a problem only arises in the case in which there is a co-operators' surplus to divide; namely, that in which the two prudential strategy lines are the two lower sides, both with negative slope, of the parallelogram which is the total strategic region. Here considerations of symmetry (e.g. that the parallelogram can be transformed into a rhombus by a utility transformation) lead me to recommend that L and M should agree to use the pure strategies which will yield the intersection of the two upper sides of the parallelogram as outcome point.

Exceptional cases in which two or more of the base points coincide may be treated by continuity considerations, as was done for the coincidence of T_{11} and T_{22} in the example at the bottom of p. 37.

1·6. In some cases the prudential isorrhope, going upwards and rightwards, intersects the boundary of the total strategic region at a point where this boundary is a straight line with positive slope. In these cases my recommended outcome point can be improved, to the benefit of both parties, by moving it upwards and rightwards along this line to the base point which ends it. The strategies to be recommended in these cases are the pure strategies represented by this base point.

70

2. *Extension to a general $n \times n$ collaboration situation*

2·1. The geometrical treatment cannot conveniently be extended to collaboration situations in which the collaborators have more than two strategies each, since the weighted strategies will not then in general be representable by lines. But the algebraic treatment of §§1·1 and 1·2 can be straightforwardly extended to an $n \times n$ situation in which each collaborator has a choice among n pure strategies, where n is any finite positive integer, the same for both parties.

For, although each of the pair of utility tables, expanded so as to allow for all weighted strategies, will have an $(n-1)$-fold infinity of rows and an $(n-1)$-fold infinity of columns, each will in general include a four-square core. (The strategies involved in the pair of cores will be representable geometrically by a horizontal and a vertical line.) As in the 2×2 situation, the cores will specify 'natural units' of L-utility and of M-utility which can be used to fix the direction of the isorrhopic beam; and the argument of the lecture can then proceed exactly as in the 2×2 case.

2·2. Let the L-utility table $\mathbf{X}$ be the $n \times n$ square array representing, in values of x, the L-utilities a_{rs}, with the row index $r = 1, 2, ..., n$; the column index $s = 1, 2, ..., n$. Let the M-utility table $\mathbf{Y}$ be the $n \times n$ square array representing, in values of y, the M-utilities b_{rs}, with $r, s = 1, 2, ..., n$. Then L's choice of his pure strategy $L_r (r = 1, 2, ..., n)$ may be represented by choice of the rth row, and M's choice of his pure strategy M_s ($s = 1, 2, ..., n$) represented by choice of the sth column, in both these tables.

If $\mathbf{Z}$ is any square array, denote by $\mathbf{Z}^T$ the square array obtained by interchanging rows with columns in $\mathbf{Z}$ (i.e. $\mathbf{Z}^T$ is the *transpose* of $\mathbf{Z}$). Denote by $\Delta(\mathbf{Z})$ the determinant of $\mathbf{Z}$, and by $\Gamma(\mathbf{Z})$ the sum of all the co-factors of elements of $\Delta(\mathbf{Z})$. $\Delta(\mathbf{Z}) = \Delta(\mathbf{Z}^T)$, and $\Gamma(\mathbf{Z}) = \Gamma(\mathbf{Z}^T)$.

For an $n \times n$ collaboration situation a *weighted strategy* $L(W)$ or $M(W)$ is one determined by a weight-vector $W = \{w_1, w_2, ..., w_n\}$ in which each pure strategy L_r, M_r respectively is weighted with a weight-factor of w_r, w_r being the rth component of the weight-vector W, and where the components of the vector satisfy the equation $\sum_r w_r = 1$.* (For $n = 2$ this reduces to the explanation of §1·1 by taking the $L(w)$ and $M(w)$ of §1·1 as $L(W)$ and $M(W)$ respectively, with $W = \{1 - w, w\}$.)

The equalizing weight-vectors C, D, E, F determining respectively the equalizing strategies $L(C)$, $L(D)$, $M(E)$, $M(F)$ have components whose values, together with the values of the L-utilities c_0, e_0 obtained by the use of $L(C)$, $M(E)$ respectively and of the M-utilities d_0, f_0 obtained by the use of $L(D)$, $M(F)$ respectively, are solutions of the four sets each of $n + 1$ simultaneous equations

$$\sum_i c_i = 1, \quad \sum_i a_{is} c_i = c_0 \quad \text{for} \quad s = 1, 2, ..., n;$$

$$\sum_i d_i = 1, \quad \sum_i b_{is} d_i = d_0 \quad \text{for} \quad s = 1, 2, ..., n;$$

$$\sum_j e_j = 1, \quad \sum_j a_{rj} e_j = e_0 \quad \text{for} \quad r = 1, 2, ..., n;$$

$$\sum_j f_j = 1, \quad \sum_j b_{rj} f_j = f_0 \quad \text{for} \quad r = 1, 2, ..., n.$$

Necessary and sufficient conditions for these four sets of simultaneous equations to have unique solutions are: for the first set, $\Gamma(\mathbf{X}^T) \neq 0$; for the second set, $\Gamma(\mathbf{Y}^T) \neq 0$; for the third set, $\Gamma(\mathbf{X}) \neq 0$; for the fourth set, $\Gamma(\mathbf{Y}) \neq 0$.

Now suppose $\Gamma(\mathbf{X}) \neq 0$, $\Gamma(\mathbf{Y}) \neq 0$. Then $\Gamma(\mathbf{X}^T) \neq 0$, $\Gamma(\mathbf{Y}^T) \neq 0$, and all the conditions are satisfied.

Solving the sets of equations for c_0, d_0, e_0, f_0 gives

$$c_0 = e_0 = \frac{\Delta(\mathbf{X})}{\Gamma(\mathbf{X})}, \quad d_0 = f_0 = \frac{\Delta(\mathbf{Y})}{\Gamma(\mathbf{Y})}.$$

* All summations denoted by Σ will be understood to be over n terms.

Inspection of the equations shows that C, D, E, F are invariant with respect to any linear transformation of the a's of $\mathbf{X}$ and of the b's of $\mathbf{Y}$. The algebra will be simplified if we transform the a's and the b's respectively by the utility transformations

$$\xi = x - \frac{\Delta(\mathbf{X})}{\Gamma(\mathbf{X})}, \quad \eta = y - \frac{\Delta(\mathbf{Y})}{\Gamma(\mathbf{Y})}.$$

(These transformations are equivalent geometrically to taking the vertical line representing the two L-utility-equalizing strategies and the horizontal line representing the two M-utility-equalizing strategies as the vertical and horizontal axes of the ξ, η plane.) α's in an array Ξ and β's in an array $\mathbf{H}$ will be used to denote the new values of the L-utilities (values of ξ) and of the M-utilities (values of η) respectively.

The transformed sets of equations are the original sets with α's and β's substituted for the a's and b's, and with o substituted for c_0, d_0, e_0, f_0. Since $\Delta(\Xi) = $ o and $\Delta(\mathbf{H}) = $ o, the solutions for C, D, E, F are given by the following sets of equalities, where A_{ij} denotes the cofactor of α_{ij} in $\Delta(\Xi)$ and B_{ij} the co-factor of β_{ij} in $\Delta(\mathbf{H})$, so that $\Gamma(\Xi) = \sum_i \sum_j A_{ij}$, $\Gamma(\mathbf{H}) = \sum_i \sum_j B_{ij}$:

$$c_r = \frac{A_{r1}}{\sum_i A_{i1}} = \frac{A_{r2}}{\sum_i A_{i2}} = \ldots = \frac{A_{rn}}{\sum_i A_{in}} = \frac{\sum_j A_{rj}}{\Gamma(\Xi)} \quad \text{for every } r;$$

$$d_r = \frac{B_{r1}}{\sum_i B_{i1}} = \frac{B_{r2}}{\sum_i B_{i2}} = \ldots = \frac{B_{rn}}{\sum_i B_{in}} = \frac{\sum_j B_{rj}}{\Gamma(\mathbf{H})} \quad \text{for every } r;$$

$$e_s = \frac{A_{1s}}{\sum_j A_{1j}} = \frac{A_{2s}}{\sum_j A_{2j}} = \ldots = \frac{A_{ns}}{\sum_j A_{nj}} = \frac{\sum_i A_{is}}{\Gamma(\Xi)} \quad \text{for every } s;$$

$$f_s = \frac{B_{1s}}{\sum_j B_{1j}} = \frac{B_{2s}}{\sum_j B_{2j}} = \ldots = \frac{B_{ns}}{\sum_j B_{nj}} = \frac{\sum_i B_{is}}{\Gamma(\mathbf{H})} \quad \text{for every } s.$$

All the denominators in these fractions are different from o, since the vector components are solutions of the untransformed equations in the a's and b's, which have unique solutions when $\Gamma(\mathbf{X}) \neq \mathrm{o}$, $\Gamma(\mathbf{Y}) \neq \mathrm{o}$.

The L-utility (value of ξ) resulting from both L and M using their M-utility-equalizing strategies $L(D)$, $M(F)$ respectively will be

$$\sum_r \sum_s \alpha_{rs} d_r f_s = \sum_r \sum_s \alpha_{rs} \left(\frac{B_{rs}}{\sum_i B_{is}} \right) \left(\frac{\sum_i B_{is}}{\Gamma(\mathbf{H})} \right) = \frac{\mathrm{I}}{\Gamma(\mathbf{H})} \sum_r \sum_s \alpha_{rs} B_{rs}.$$

The M-utility (value of η) resulting from both L and M using their L-utility-equalizing strategies $L(C)$, $M(E)$ respectively will be

$$\sum_r \sum_s \beta_{rs} c_r e_s = \sum_r \sum_s \beta_{rs} \left(\frac{A_{rs}}{\sum_i A_{is}} \right) \left(\frac{\sum_i A_{is}}{\Gamma(\Xi)} \right) = \frac{\mathrm{I}}{\Gamma(\Xi)} \sum_r \sum_s \beta_{rs} A_{rs}.$$

So the cores of the utility tables in the Ξ, $\mathbf{H}$ representation are

	L-utility core (values of ξ)			M-utility core (values of η)	
	$M(E)$	$M(F)$		$M(E)$	$M(F)$
$L(C)$	o	o	$L(C)$	$\dfrac{\sum_r \sum_s \beta_{rs} A_{rs}}{\sum_r \sum_s A_{rs}}$	o
$L(D)$	o	$\dfrac{\sum_r \sum_s \alpha_{rs} B_{rs}}{\sum_r \sum_s B_{rs}}$	$L(D)$	o	o

Thus the 'natural units' of L-utility and of M-utility in the Ξ, $\mathbf{H}$ representation and also in the $\mathbf{X}$, $\mathbf{Y}$ representa-

74

tion will be the absolute values of $\dfrac{\sum\limits_{r}\sum\limits_{s}\alpha_{rs}B_{rs}}{\sum\limits_{r}\sum\limits_{s}B_{rs}}$ and of

$\dfrac{\sum\limits_{r}\sum\limits_{s}\beta_{rs}A_{rs}}{\sum\limits_{r}\sum\limits_{s}A_{rs}}$ respectively.

2·3. The method for finding the strategies, or coupled strategy, to be recommended can now proceed exactly as in a 2 × 2 situation. The L-utilities and the M-utilities can be rescaled by the utility transformations

$$u = \left| \dfrac{\sum\limits_{r}\sum\limits_{s}B_{rs}}{\sum\limits_{r}\sum\limits_{s}\alpha_{rs}B_{rs}} \right| \xi, \quad v = \left| \dfrac{\sum\limits_{r}\sum\limits_{s}A_{rs}}{\sum\limits_{r}\sum\limits_{s}\beta_{rs}A_{rs}} \right| \eta$$

respectively, and the prudential isorrhope can then be specified as the line of slope 1 in the u, v plane which passes through the outcome point which is the 'solution' of the zero-sum 'relative game' in $u-v$. The recommendation to L and M will be to use such strategies, or such a coupled strategy, as will secure as outcome point the intersection of the prudential isorrhope, continued upwards and rightwards, with the convex polygon which is the boundary of the total strategic region (or a vertex of the polygon obtained by improving on the recommendation in the manner of §1·6).

Although the amount of numerical calculation involved increases very rapidly with increasing n, the recommendation resulting therefrom is as simple in a general $n \times n$ collaboration situation as in a general 2 × 2 situation; namely, one of the three alternatives: (1) to use a conjunction of two pure strategies, one for each party; (2) to use a conjunction of a pure strategy of one party with a mixed strategy of the other; (3) to use a probability combination of a conjunction of two pure strategies, one for each party, with a conjunction of

75

another two pure strategies, one for each party. That the alternatives are the same whatever be the value of n (provided that $n \geqslant 2$) arises from the two facts that the boundary of a total strategic region is always a convex *polygon* and that the co-ordinates of a point on the side of a polygon are convex linear combinations of the co-ordinates of the *two* neighbouring vertices.